MW01126653

OPTIMIZING AN OCTOPUS

For Ethan and Logan,
There is an
engineer in all
of us! Michelle Pantoya
2019

AN ENGINEERING EVERYTHING ADVENTURE

OPTIMIZING AN OCTOPUS

EMILY HUNT AND MICHELLE PANTOYA

BOOK TWO IN
ENGINEERING EVERYTHING

ILLUSTRATED BY

LAURA JONES MARTINEZ

TEXAS TECH UNIVERSITY PRESS

THIS BOOK IS TYPESET IN CREATIVE BLOCK BB. THE PAPER USED IN THIS BOOK
MEETS THE MINIMUM REQUIREMENTS OF ANSI/NISO Z39.48-1992 (R1997) ∞

DESIGNED BY LAURA JONES MARTINEZ
COVER ILLUSTRATION BY LAURA JONES MARTINEZ

LIBRARY OF CONGRESS CATALOGING-IN-PUBLICATION NUMBER:
2017945190

PRINTED IN THE UNITED STATES OF AMERICA
18 19 20 21 22 23 24 25 26 / 9 8 7 6 5 4 3 2 1

TEXAS TECH UNIVERSITY PRESS
BOX 41037
LUBBOCK, TEXAS 79409-1037 USA
800-832-4042
TTUP@TTU.EDU
WWW.TTUPRESS.ORG

OPTIMIZING
AN OCTOPUS

3

THREE DAYS AGO, ON PLANET EXERGY

AS YOU KNOW, WE EXERGONS ARE FACED WITH WILDLIFE MOVING INTO OUR CITIES.

EXERGY DEFENSE COUNCIL

MANY SPECIES ARE SO LARGE THAT WE FEAR THEY SEE US AS FOOD.

4

6

LATER THAT DAY IN THE LAB

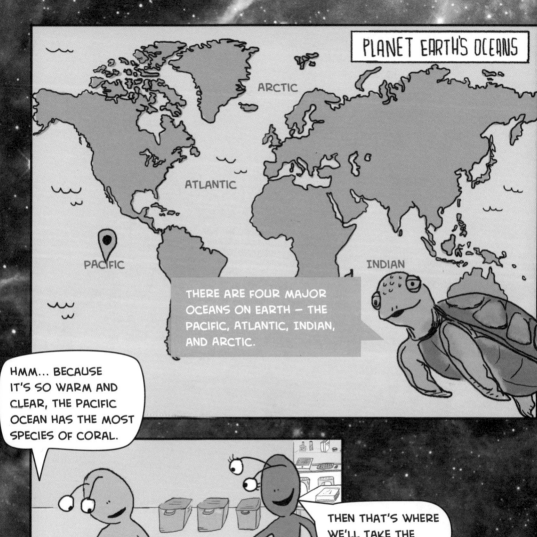

WELL, IT CERTAINLY LOOKS SHARP ENOUGH TO REPEL INVADERS.

WHAT DO YOU THINK, BELLS? COULD STUDYING A CORAL REEF HELP US PROTECT OUR CITIES?

CORAL IS NOT ONLY RAZOR SHARP BUT SOMETIMES DEADLY TOXIC TO THE TOUCH.

12

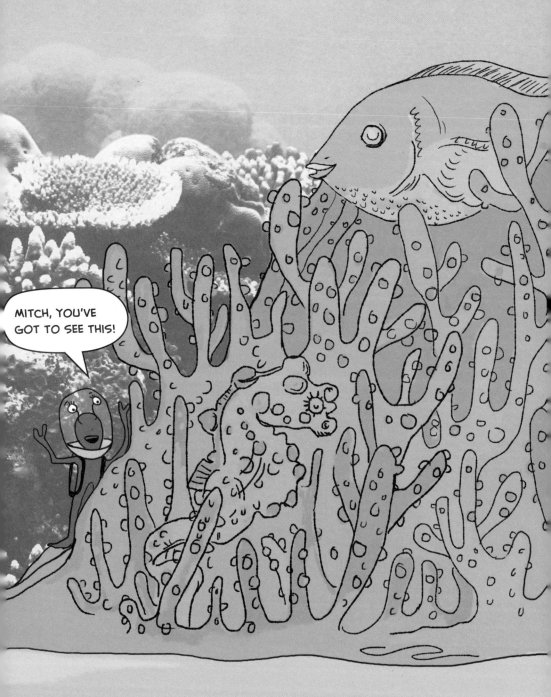

15

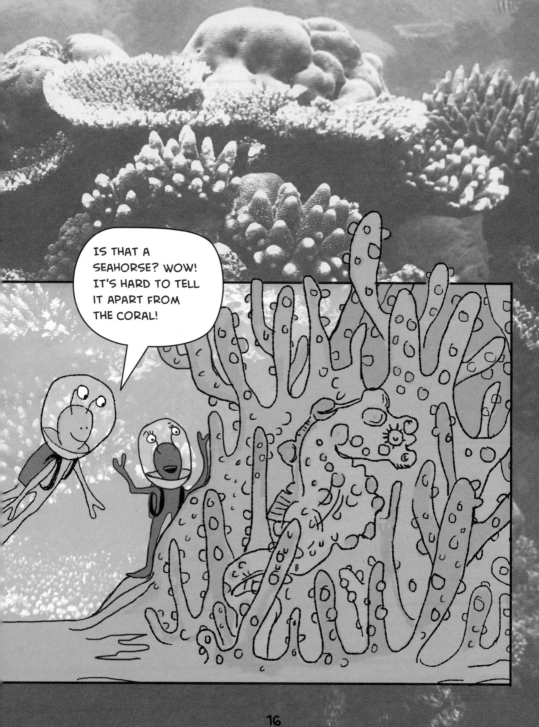

19

OCTOPUS EGGS CAN TAKE TEN MONTHS TO HATCH. A MOTHER OCTOPUS PROTECTS HER EGGS FIERCELY.

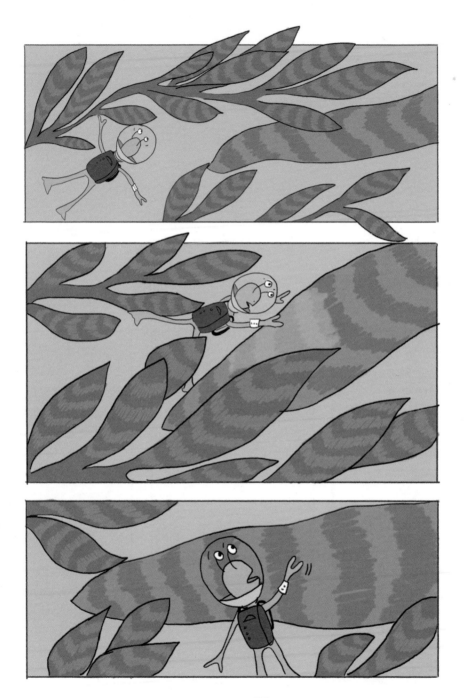

LIKE THE OCTOPUS, THE SQUID IS A CEPHALOPOD AND MASTER OF DISGUISE.

WHOA! THIS GIANT FROND IS REALLY A SQUID ARM? CAN EVERYTHING IN THE OCEAN DISGUISE ITSELF?

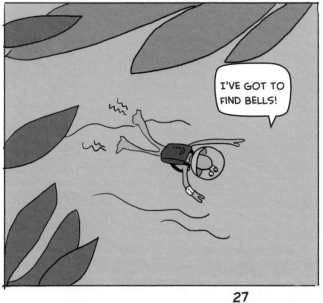

I'VE GOT TO FIND BELLS!

LIKE THE SQUID, THE OCTOPUS CAN HIDE IN PLAIN SIGHT. SOME CEPHALOPODS USE PIGMENT CELLS AND MUSCLES THAT ALLOW THEIR SKIN TO MIMIC SURROUNDING COLORS, PATTERNS, AND TEXTURES.

LOOK—THERE'S A SHARK! HE DOESN'T EVEN NOTICE THE OCTOPUS.

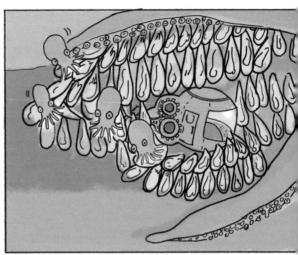

35

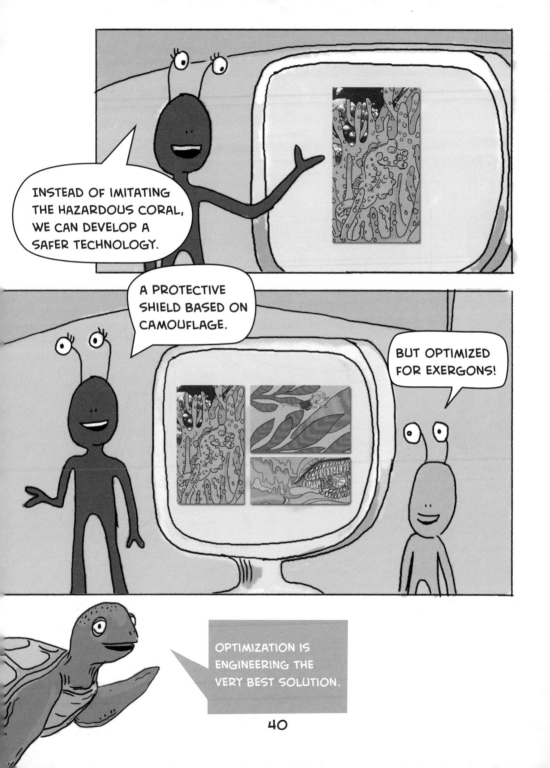

40

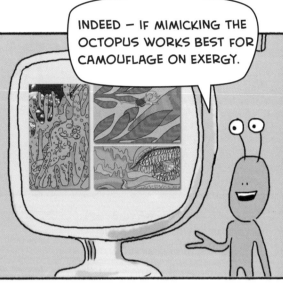

42

43

ASK

WHICH TYPE OF CAMOUFLAGE WILL WORK THE BEST?

WE LEARN SO MUCH BY OBSERVING!

ALWAYS FASCINATING, ISN'T IT?

THEY ARE STUDYING HOW THE CEPHALOPODS' CAMOUFLAGE WORKS AND THINKING ABOUT HOW TO MIMIC CAMOUFLAGE.

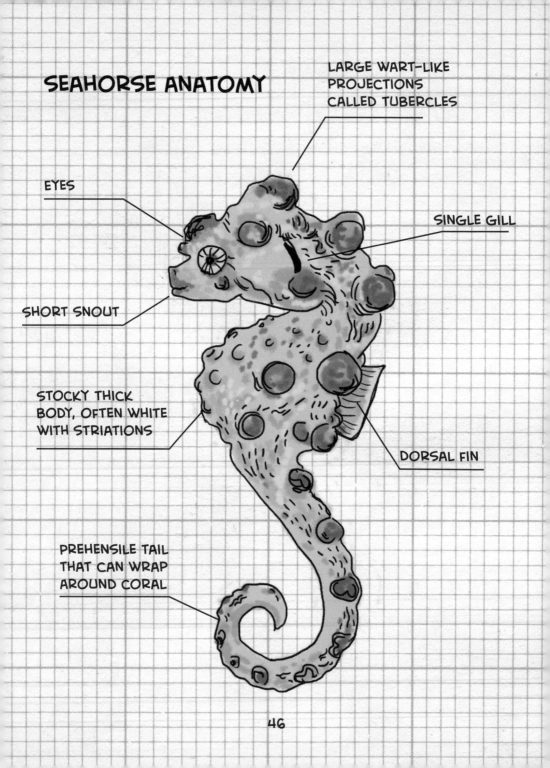

SEAHORSE ANATOMY

LARGE WART-LIKE
PROJECTIONS
CALLED TUBERCLES

EYES

SINGLE GILL

SHORT SNOUT

STOCKY THICK
BODY, OFTEN WHITE
WITH STRIATIONS

DORSAL FIN

PREHENSILE TAIL
THAT CAN WRAP
AROUND CORAL

HOW DOES THE SEAHORSE CAMOUFLAGE ITSELF?

A PYGMY SEAHORSE BLENDS SWIFTLY INTO ITS HABITAT BY:

1. USING THOUSANDS OF CHROMATOPHORES, SAC-LIKE ORGANELLES THAT CONTAIN MOSTLY PURPLE, RED, AND YELLOW PIGMENT.

2. PUSHING THOSE SACS CLOSER OR FARTHER FROM THE SURFACE OF ITS SKIN, DEPENDING ON THE COLORS NEEDED.

3. REPRESSING THOSE COLOR SACS TO CREATE A REFLECTIVE WHITE SURFACE.

4. CHANGING THE COLOR OF ITS SKIN AND TUBERCLES TO MATCH ITS HOST CORAL.

OCTOPUS ANATOMY

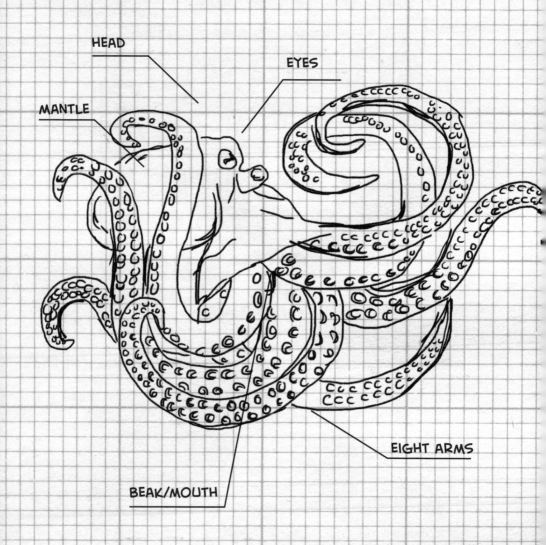

HEAD

EYES

MANTLE

EIGHT ARMS

BEAK/MOUTH

48

HOW DOES THE OCTOPUS CAMOUFLAGE ITSELF?

THE OCTOPUS BLENDS SWIFTLY INTO ITS HABITAT BY:

1. USING MILLIONS OF CHROMATOPHORES, ORGANS CONTAINING SACS OF BROWN, BLACK, RED, ORANGE, OR YELLOW PIGMENT.
2. USING LEUCOPHORES AND IRIDOPHORES – CELLS CONTAINING REFLECTORS – THAT CREATE GREENS, BLUES, AND WHITES.
3. RELAXING AND CONTRACTING MUSCLES AROUND ITS CHROMATOPHORES TO PRODUCE SKIN PATTERNS WITH COLORS, SHADES, AND CONTRAST.
4. RAISING SKIN POINTS CALLED PAPILLAE TO IMITATE NEARBY TEXTURES.
5. ADJUSTING ITS FLEXIBLE SOFT BODY TO ALTER ITS SHAPE AND BETTER CONCEAL ITSELF AND ITS EGGS.

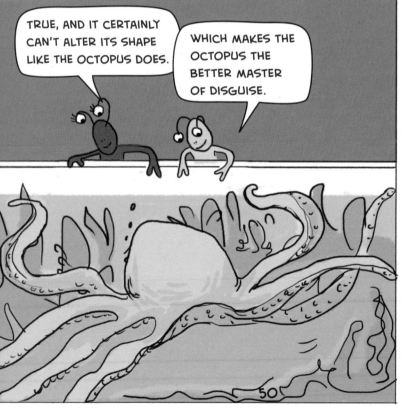

50

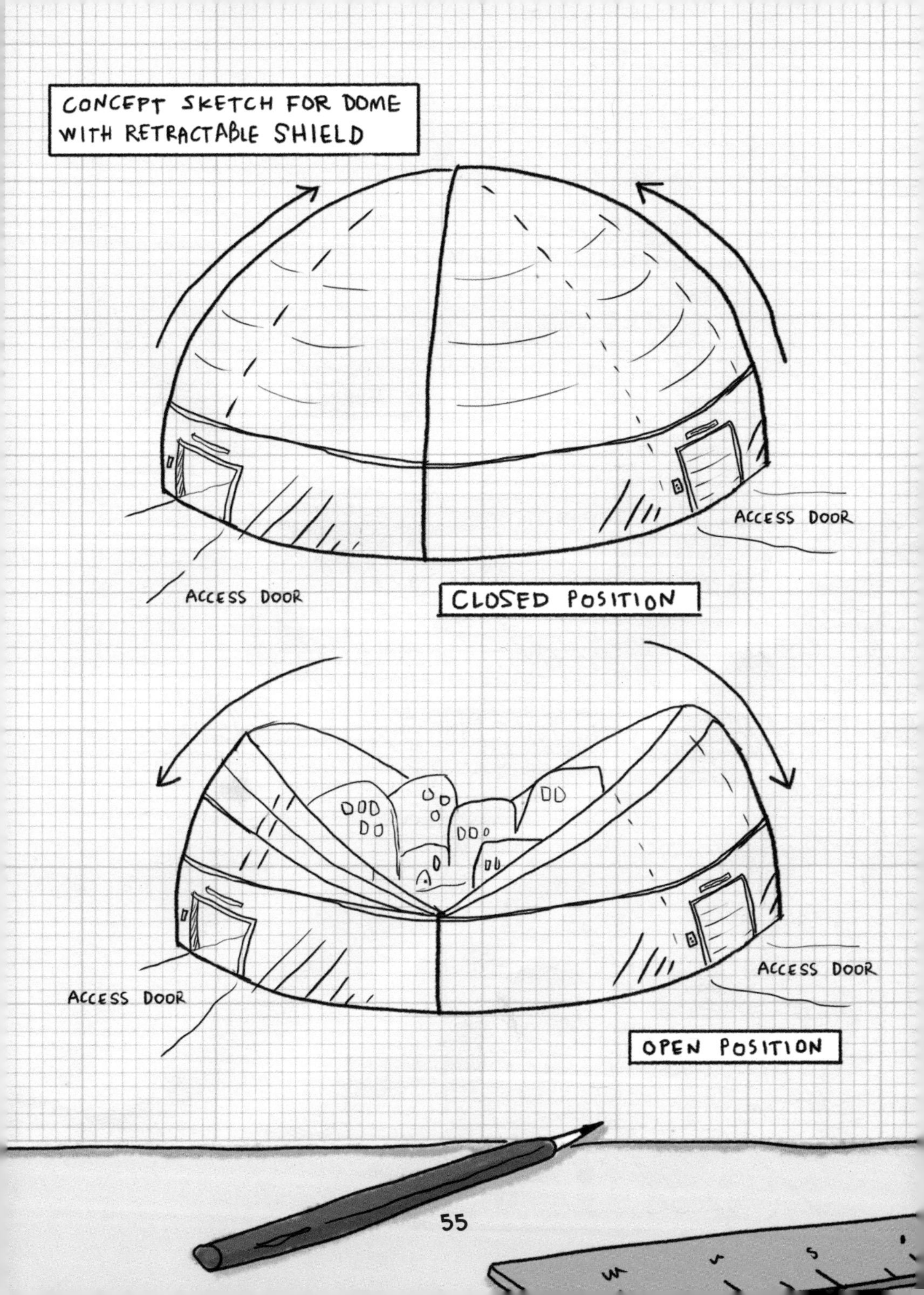

CONCEPT SKETCH FOR DOME WITH RETRACTABLE SHIELD

ACCESS DOOR

ACCESS DOOR

CLOSED POSITION

ACCESS DOOR

ACCESS DOOR

OPEN POSITION

55

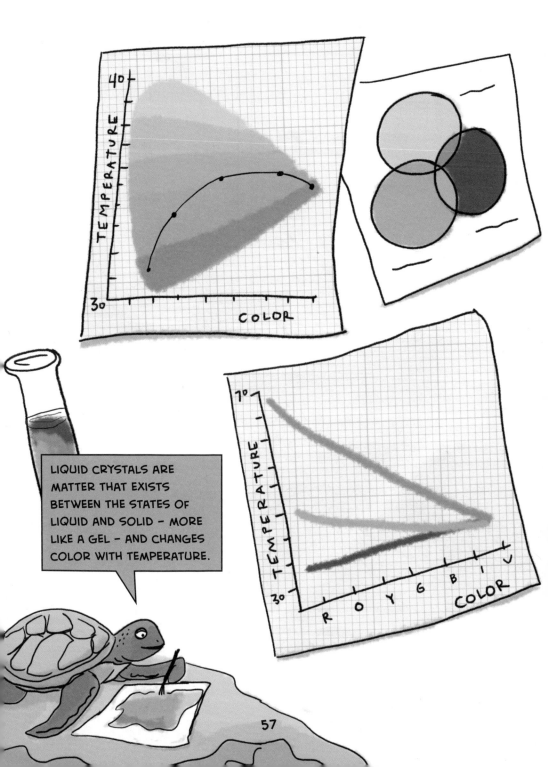

LIQUID CRYSTALS ARE MATTER THAT EXISTS BETWEEN THE STATES OF LIQUID AND SOLID – MORE LIKE A GEL – AND CHANGES COLOR WITH TEMPERATURE.

59

62

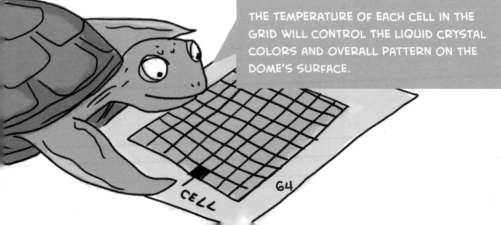

64

THE DEFENSE COUNCIL SHOULD **LOVE** IT.

74

75

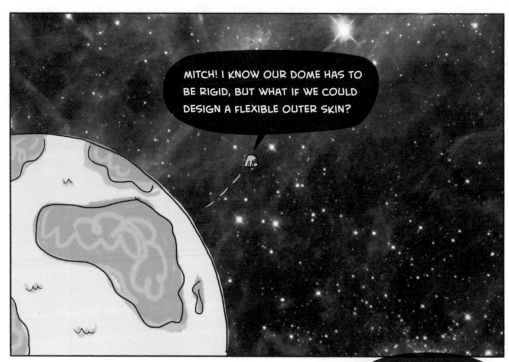

GLOSSARY

CAMOUFLAGE (N.): HIDING OR DISGUISING BY BLENDING IN WITH THE SURROUNDINGS.

CELL (N.): THE SMALLEST STRUCTURAL UNIT WITHIN A GRID.

CEPHALOPOD (N.): A MARINE MOLLUSK THAT MOVES BY EXPELLING WATER FROM A TUBULAR SIPHON UNDER THE HEAD AND HAS A GROUP OF SUCKER-BEARING ARMS (OR TENTACLES) AROUND THE HEAD. INCLUDES THE CUTTLEFISH, SQUID, AND OCTOPUS.

CHROMATOPHORES (N.): PIGMENT-CONTAINING AND LIGHT-REFLECTING CELLS THAT ARE FOUND IN A WIDE RANGE OF ANIMALS, INCLUDING AMPHIBIANS, FISH, REPTILES, CRUSTACEANS, AND CEPHALOPODS. IN CONTRAST, MAMMALS AND BIRDS HAVE A CLASS OF CELLS CALLED MELANOCYTES FOR COLORATION.

DORSAL FIN (N.): AN UNPAIRED FIN ON THE BACK OF A FISH OR WHALE.

ENGINEER (N.): A PERSON WHO USES SCIENCE AND MATH TO DESIGN NEW TECHNOLOGIES OR TO DESIGN IMPROVEMENTS FOR EXISTING TECHNOLOGIES.

FORCE (N.): A PUSH OR PULL UPON AN OBJECT RESULTING FROM THE OBJECT'S INTERACTION WITH ANOTHER OBJECT. WHENEVER THERE IS AN INTERACTION BETWEEN TWO OBJECTS, THERE IS A FORCE UPON EACH OF THE OBJECTS.

FROND (N.): A LEAF OR LEAF-LIKE PART OF A PALM, FERN, OR SIMILAR PLANT.

GILLS (N.): THE PAIRED RESPIRATORY ORGAN OF FISHES AND SOME AMPHIBIANS THAT ENABLE OXYGEN TO BE EXTRACTED FROM WATER.

HABITAT (N.): A NATURAL HOME OR ENVIRONMENT OF AN ANIMAL, PLANT, OR OTHER ORGANISM.

HYDRAULICS (N.): A BRANCH OF SCIENCE AND TECHNOLOGY THAT FOCUSES ON THE MOVEMENT OF LIQUIDS THROUGH PIPES AND CHANNELS, ESPECIALLY AS A SOURCE OF MECHANICAL FORCE OR CONTROL.

HYPOTHESIS (N.): AN IDEA OR EXPLANATION THAT CAN BE TESTED THROUGH STUDY AND EXPERIMENTATION.

IMPENETRABLE (ADJ.): IMPOSSIBLE TO PASS THROUGH OR ENTER.

IRIDOPHORES (N.): AN IRIDESCENT CHROMATOPHORE SHOWING LUMINOUS COLORS THAT SEEM TO CHANGE WHEN VIEWED FROM DIFFERENT ANGLES.

LANDSLIDE (N.): MARINE LANDSLIDES TRANSPORT SEDIMENT ACROSS THE CONTINENTAL SHELF AND INTO THE DEEP OCEAN.

LEUCOPHORES (N.): ANY CHROMATOPHORE THAT SHOWS WHITE IN REFLECTED LIGHT.

MANTLE (N.): A SIGNIFICANT PART OF A MOLLUSK'S ANATOMY, CONSISTING OF A DORSAL BODY WALL THAT COVERS THE INNER MASS AND PROTRUDES OUTWARD, USUALLY IN THE FORM OF FLAPS.

PAPILLAE (N.): A SMALL, ROUND BUMP OR GROWTH ON A PART OR ORGAN OF A BODY.

POWER (N.): THE AMOUNT OF ENERGY PUT OUT OR PRODUCED IN A GIVEN AMOUNT OF TIME. POWER EQUALS ENERGY PER UNIT OF TIME AND IS MEASURED IN WATTS.

PROTOTYPE (N.): A FIRST, TYPICAL, OR PRELIMINARY MODEL OF SOMETHING FROM WHICH OTHER FORMS ARE DEVELOPED OR COPIED.

REEF (N.): A RIDGE OF JAGGED ROCK, CORAL, OR SAND JUST ABOVE OR BELOW THE SURFACE OF THE OCEAN.

RESEARCH (N.): A SYSTEMATIC INVESTIGATION OR EXPERIMENTATION AIMED AT THE DISCOVERY AND INTERPRETATION OF FACTS.

RETRACTABLE (ADJ.): ABLE TO BE DRAWN BACK OR PULLED BACK.

SNOUT (N.): A PROJECTING NOSE AND MOUTH OF AN ANIMAL.

WEIGHT (N.): A FORCE MEASUREMENT THAT INDICATES HEAVINESS, REFLECTING THE FORCE WITH WHICH A BODY IS ATTRACTED TO EARTH.

ABOUT THE AUTHORS:

MICHELLE PANTOYA IS DIRECTOR OF THE COMBUSTION LAB AND PROFESSOR OF MECHANICAL ENGINEERING AT TEXAS TECH UNIVERSITY. EMILY HUNT, DEAN AND PROFESSOR AT WEST TEXAS A&M UNIVERSITY, USES NANOTECHNOLOGY TO SOLVE PROBLEMS. EMILY, A MOTHER OF FIVE, AND MICHELLE, A MOTHER OF FOUR, HAVE EXPANDED THEIR PASSION FOR ENGINEERING BY CO-AUTHORING CHILDREN'S BOOKS.

EMILY HUNT

MICHELLE PANTOYA